ReadingWise

Comprehension Strategies That Work

Series Consultant

Diane J. Sawyer, Ph.D.
Murfree Professor of Dyslexic Studies
Middle Tennessee State University

ReadingWise 5: Comprehension Strategies That Work
ISBN 1-56420-329-8
Copyright © 2003 New Readers Press
New Readers Press
Division of ProLiteracy Worldwide
1320 Jamesville Avenue, Syracuse, New York 13210

Printed in the United States of America
9 8 7 6 5 4 3 2

All proceeds from the sale of New Readers Press materials
support literacy programs in the United States and worldwide.

Developer: Kraft & Kraft, New York, NY
Series Editor: Judi Lauber
Production Director: Heather Witt
Designer: Shelagh Clancy
Illustrations: Len Shalansky, Brian F. Wallace, James P. Wallace
Production Specialist: Alexander Jones
Cover Design: Kimbrly Koennecke

Contents

Introduction   **To the Student** **5**

Vocabulary   **Lesson 1** ◆ **Using Clues to Meaning** **6**
                Using Context Clues

        Lesson 2 ◆ **Getting the Picture** **8**
                Understanding Figurative Meanings

Reading   **Lesson 3** ◆ **Deciding How You'll Read** **10**
Strategies   *Setting a Purpose and Method*

        Lesson 4 ◆ **Asking the Right Questions** **12**
                Questioning the Text

        Lesson 5 ◆ **Checking as You Read** **14**
                Monitoring Comprehension

        Lesson 6 ◆ **Putting It in a Few Words** **16**
                Summarizing

        Lesson 7 ◆ **Putting It in Other Words** **18**
                Paraphrasing

Topic   **Lesson 8** ◆ **Deciding What It's About** **20**
                Recognizing the Topic

        Lesson 9 ◆ **Using the Topic** **22**
                Anchoring Understanding on the Topic

Main Idea   **Lesson 10** ◆ **Finding the Writer's Point** **24**
                Recognizing the Main Idea

        Lesson 11 ◆ **Using the Writer's Point** **26**
                Building on the Main Idea

Details   **Lesson 12** ◆ **Finding Useful Details** **28**
                Recognizing Significant Details

        Lesson 13 ◆ **Using Details** **30**
                Understanding the Significance of Details

Sequence   **Lesson 14** ◆ **Deciding When It Happens** **32**
                Following a Sequence

        Lesson 15 ◆ **Using Time Order** **34**
                Understanding Sequence

Cause and Effect	Lesson 16 ◆	**Deciding Why It Happens** . . . . *Recognizing Cause and Effect*	**36**
	Lesson 17 ◆	**Using Reasons** . . . . *Understanding Cause and Effect*	**38**
Classification	Lesson 18 ◆	**Finding Groups** . . . . *Recognizing Classification*	**40**
	Lesson 19 ◆	**Using Groups** . . . . *Understanding Classification*	**42**
Comparison/ Contrast	Lesson 20 ◆	**Finding Like and Unlike** . . . . *Recognizing Comparison and Contrast*	**44**
	Lesson 21 ◆	**Using What You Find** . . . . *Understanding Comparison and Contrast*	**46**
Outcomes	Lesson 22 ◆	**Guessing What Will Happen** . . . . *Predicting Outcomes*	**48**
	Lesson 23 ◆	**Using Your Prediction** . . . . *Applying Predictions of Outcome*	**50**
Conclusions	Lesson 24 ◆	**Thinking Clearly** . . . . *Drawing Conclusions*	**52**
	Lesson 25 ◆	**Using Clear Thinking** . . . . *Applying Conclusions*	**54**
Inferences	Lesson 26 ◆	**Filling Gaps** . . . . *Making Inferences*	**56**
	Lesson 27 ◆	**Using Good Guesses** . . . . *Applying Inferences*	**58**
Generalizations	Lesson 28 ◆	**Getting the Big Picture** . . . . *Making Generalizations*	**60**
	Lesson 29 ◆	**Checking the Big Picture** . . . . *Testing Generalizations*	**62**
Facts and Opinions	Lesson 30 ◆	**Finding the Facts** . . . . *Separating Fact from Opinion*	**64**
	Lesson 31 ◆	**Thinking about Opinions** . . . . *Evaluating Opinions*	**66**
		Answer Key	**68**

To the Student

Welcome to *ReadingWise 5*.

This book will help you understand and remember more of what you read.

Good readers think when they read. This book is about the thinking skills they use.

Life has already taught you a wide range of thinking skills. This book will show you how to use them for reading.

ReadingWise 5 has 31 lessons. Each lesson builds one skill and has four parts:
- This Is the Idea tells what skill you will learn.
- Take a Closer Look shows how to use the skill.
- Try It helps you use the skill.
- Use It lets you use the skill on your own.

Adults need to read many things every day. This book includes
- news and sports reports
- opinion columns
- charts and graphs
- ads
- rules and directions
- how-to tips
- tables of contents
- texts in history, science, nature, and language
- and other things

As you read these things, *ReadingWise* helps you practice thinking skills. And these skills will help you become a better reader.

Using Clues to Meaning

◆ *Using Context Clues*

A writer may define or explain a word right in the text. A writer might use a synonym, another word that means almost the same thing. These are context clues, or hints that help you figure out a word's meaning.

This Is the Idea

Read this part of a news story and decide what debris is.

The Big Clean-Up

Today residents can begin to clean up the debris left by the flood. Wear rubber gloves during the clean-up. Some of the mud and garbage contains germs. Chemicals may have spilled during the flood, so treat all trash carefully. Scrub your hands thoroughly when you are done.

What does the word *debris* mean here? If you look at context clues, you will see that the writer uses *debris* and *mud and garbage* in the same way. The writer also mentions trash. From this, you can guess that *debris* is the mess left behind.

Take a Closer Look

Read this part of a history text and decide what calico is.

Housing in the 1850s

Gold-rush miners in California lived in a variety of housing. The luckier people lived in large tents or log cabins. Often, calico sheets hung from the ceilings. These sheets divided the room into private sections. Miners who were less lucky lived in houses made of pine branches. The branches were covered with old calico shirts, which kept out some of the wind.

What to look for

- A diadem is a crown or tiara.
- diadem, which is a crown or tiara
- a diadem, or crown,
- a diadem, a crown,
- the diadem— the crown—

Circle your answers.

1. What is made from calico?
   a. tents and cabins   b. sheets and shirts

2. What is calico?
   a. a kind of wood   b. a kind of cloth

Try It

Read this notice and decide what salmonella is.

Prevent Food Poisoning!

All food workers must wash their hands before leaving. This will reduce the risk of spreading salmonella, a common cause of food poisoning. This germ can be spread from people to food. Food that has been infected does not look spoiled, but it can make people sick.

Circle your answers.

1. What is this notice about?
   a. food poisoning
   b. food workers

2. What is salmonella?
   a. a kind of food
   b. a kind of germ

Use It

As you read, decide what the Preamble is and what *ratify* means.

The United States Constitution

The Constitution is a written document that explains the basic ideas the U.S. government is based on. Its Preamble—the first paragraph—gives a summary of these ideas. A group of people wrote this document in 1787. Then each state had to ratify, or accept, it as law. This took several more years.

Circle your answers.

1. What is this text about?
   a. The U.S. Constitution
   b. the Preamble

2. What is the Constitution?
   a. a paragraph
   b. a written document

3. What is the Preamble?
   a. a group of people
   b. the first paragraph

4. What does *ratify* mean?
   a. to accept
   b. to write

Getting the Picture

◆ *Understanding Figurative Meanings*

Writers often use words to create images. Sometimes the words say one thing but mean something else. (If you're "climbing the walls," you're upset, but you're not really crawling up the walls.) Words used this way are called *figures of speech*.

This Is the Idea

As you read this art review, look for words that mean something different from what they say. Look for figures of speech.

A Show Worth Visiting

Ms. Gallo makes familiar scenes look fresh through her use of colors. Her reds and blues almost leap off the canvas, drawing your eyes where she wants you to look. Her best picture has an explosion of color in the center that turns out to be a bouquet of flowers.

The paints in a painting do not really jump off a canvas or explode. But if something did leap off a painting, it would draw your attention. When you picture an explosion, do you picture a bright flash of light and color? Perhaps this is what the bouquet of flowers looks like.

Take a Closer Look

To understand figures of speech

- If the simple meanings of the words don't make sense, think about what *would* make sense.

As you read this parenting tip, look for figures of speech.

Getting Your Teens to Talk to You

Do you complain that your teens don't talk to you? Try putting yourself in your kids' shoes, and you may learn why. Do you really listen to them, or do you lecture them? Do you bite their heads off when they make mistakes?

1. Circle what "putting yourself in your kids' shoes" probably means.
   a. seeing things their way   b. wearing their sneakers
2. Circle what "bite their heads off" probably means.
   a. admire them   b. attack them

Try It

As you read this part of a letter, look for figures of speech.

Dear Belle,

Last night the City Council met to decide whether to build a new school in our district. As you can imagine, the kids and I have been on pins and needles waiting for this decision. The final vote was positive, so we will get a new school. When Mr. Wong announced the vote, it was music to my ears.

Write your answers.

1. If you were on pins and needles, would you feel tense or relaxed?

_____

2. When the writer says "it was music to my ears," what does this suggest? Was the writer pleased with the vote or unhappy with it?

_____

Use It

As you read this advice, look for figures of speech.

Improve Your Storage

If your closets are bursting at the seams and your heart sinks at the prospect of finding space for new purchases, you need to rearrange your storage. First, you should weed out those items that you seldom use, and then move other items close to where you actually use them.

Write your answers.

1. Is a closet "bursting at the seams" likely to be stuffed full or empty?

_____

2. If "your heart sinks," do you feel excited or discouraged?

_____

3. What figure of speech does the writer use to mean "get rid of"?

_____

Deciding How You'll Read

◆ *Setting a Purpose and Method*

This Is the Idea

Decide why and how you would read the rest of this news report.

Drought Emergency in Effect

CENTER CITY — The mayor's office has issued a drought emergency. That means that water-saving rules are in effect. (The complete water-saving rules are listed on page 4.) Rainfall has been below normal for six months in a row. This is the longest drought in 20 years.

Sometimes you read to get just the information you need. This report is about a drought and water-saving rules. You may want to know the whole story. But if you just want to know the rules, you will turn to page 4 and read quickly to know what you should do.

Take a Closer Look

Decide why and how you would read the rest of this sports feature.

What to do

- To understand something in depth, read slowly.
- To find just the facts you need, read quickly.
- To help yourself remember, take notes.

Marathon Results

More runners competed in this year's Center City Marathon than in any previous year in the race's 12-year history. The weather could not have been better—not too hot, not too cold, and not too wet. The course led from Memorial Park along the river and over Rocky Hill to finish at City Hall.

You might read the feature slowly to understand something in depth or quickly to find a fact. Check two reasons why someone would read the feature quickly.

_____ a. to learn who won the race

_____ b. to find out exactly how the race went, mile by mile

_____ c. to find out the winning time in the race

Try It

Why and how would you read chapters in this book?

Contents

Chapter 1. The History of Yellowstone ....

Chapter 2. Where to Stay When Visiting Yellowstone....

Chapter 3. The Animals of Yellowstone.......................

Chapter 4. The Birds of Yellowstone ....

Circle your answers.

1. Why would someone read Chapter 2 quickly?
   a. to find out how large Yellowstone National Park is
   b. to find a motel near Yellowstone National Park

2. Why would someone read Chapter 1 slowly and carefully?
   a. to find out if Yellowstone National Park is in Wyoming
   b. to find out how Yellowstone became a national park

Use It

Why and how would you read this special section of a newspaper?

Candidates on the Issues

We asked all the local candidates to answer questions about the key issues this year. Each of their answers is in this special section. The candidates are listed in order by the position for which they are running.

Write your answers.

1. You want to find out who is running for city council in your district. Will you read this special section quickly or slowly?

   _____

2. You want to compare all the candidates' plans for the city's schools. Will you read this special section quickly or slowly?

   _____

Asking the Right Questions

◆ *Questioning the Text*

Asking questions about the text helps you understand what you read. Asking questions helps you identify the most important parts of the text.

This Is the Idea

As you read this advice to parents, ask "How?"

KEEP YOUR TODDLER SAFE

Once babies start to crawl and walk, you have to take special care to keep them safe. Be especially careful about falls and poisons. Place gates at the tops and bottoms of stairs. Do not use the older kind that can trap a child's head. Make sure that all drugs, cleaning supplies, and poisons are out of reach.

To find out how you can keep your toddler safe, look for the word *safe* in the text. Keep asking "How?" and you will learn just how you can keep your child safe.

Take a Closer Look

As you read this art text, ask "Who? What? Why?"

Ask
- Who?
- What?
- When?
- Where?
- How?
- Why?

The New Acrylics

Created by chemists, acrylic paints became quite popular with artists because the paints could be used in so many ways. They combined some of the best qualities of oils and watercolors. Acrylics could be applied as bright globs of color or as a transparent wash.

Write your answers.

1. Who created acrylic paints?

_____

2. Why did artists like acrylic paints? *Hint:* How were acrylics different from other paints?

_____

Try It

Read this part of an article. Ask yourself questions about it.

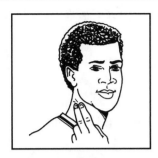

Checking Your Heart Rate

If you exercise to strengthen your heart, you should check your pulse rate often. An easy place to feel your pulse is on the side of your neck, just below your jawbone. If you're a healthy person of 25, try to get your heart beating about 100 beats a minute. Older people should aim for a slower rate. After you've been working out for a few weeks, you can slowly raise the rate.

Write your answers.

1. Where is a good place to check your pulse?

_____

2. When can you raise the rate above 100 beats a minute?

_____

Use It

Read this part of a computer text. Ask yourself questions about it.

THE NET

The Internet is a network of computer networks. These networks are linked to each other, often by cables or phone wires. The Internet allows all the computers in these networks to communicate with one another. Anyone who is linked can send files, pictures, or music to someone else who is on the Internet.

Write your answers.

1. What is the Internet?

_____

2. How are computer networks linked to form the Internet?

_____

3. What does the Internet allow computers to do?

_____

4. Who can send files and pictures to someone else on the Internet?

_____

Checking as You Read

Use a chart to check your understanding as you read. First, recall what you already know about the subject. Then decide what you want to know about it. As you read, note what you learn.

This Is the Idea

Read the title and cover of this book. Decide what it will be about.

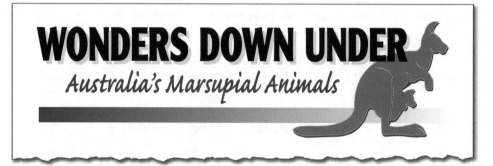

You can tell that this book will be about animals in Australia. You may not know the word *marsupial*. The picture of a kangaroo helps you. What do you already know about them? What would you like to learn?

Take a Closer Look

Jin made this chart about Australia's animals. Read the information on it.

What I Already Know	What I Want to Know	What I Learned
Kangaroo has a pouch where mother carries young.	Heard of the wallaby, but don't know what it is.	
Kangaroo has strong hind legs.	What do kangaroos eat?	

1. Copy one thing that Jin already knows about Australia's animals.

   _____

2. Copy one thing that Jin wants to know about Australia's animals.

   _____

Try It

Look at this chart about these animals, and decide what should go on it.

What I Already Know	What I Want to Know	What I Learned

1. Let's say that you already know this about these animals. Put it on the chart.

   The wallaby is about the size of a rabbit.

2. Let's say that you want to know this about these animals. Put it on the chart.

   How do the young get into the mother's pouch?

3. Add something else that you already know about these animals.

4. Add something else that you want to know about these animals.

Use It

Now read this part of the book to learn more about these animals.
What new facts do you learn about them?

Female marsupials (mar-SOO-pee-uls) have pouches where their young live until they are old enough to stop nursing. Right after birth, the young marsupial crawls to its mother's pouch.

The largest Australian marsupial is the kangaroo. The wallaby is like a kangaroo, but smaller—about the size of a rabbit.

The koala, which lives in trees, resembles a living teddy bear. The wombat looks something like a tiny bear and lives in a burrow.

All these marsupials eat plants, although some other marsupials are meat-eaters. Wombats are sometimes kept as pets.

Add the things you learned to the chart above.

Putting It in a Few Words

◆ *Summarizing*

Summarizing can help you remember what you've read. Summarize what you read by putting it into a few words. As you read, pause now and then to sum up what you've read.

This Is the Idea

How would you summarize this travel tip?

Copy Those Credit Cards

Visiting a copy center before a trip can save you trouble if your wallet is lost or stolen. Make photocopies of all your credit cards. Just lay them face down on a copier and copy. Then turn them over and copy the other side. Now all your credit card numbers are recorded in one place. Keep the copies in a safe place, and *not* in your wallet.

You could summarize the most important parts of this tip: "Before you travel, make copies of your credit cards. Keep the copies in a safe place."

Take a Closer Look

Read this part of an article and summarize it in your mind.

Who Invented Golf?

Scotland is generally said to be the birthplace of golf, but there is no firm proof that it was. People in early Rome played a game much like golf. Hundreds of years ago, a similar game was played in Holland and Denmark. In Holland, it was called kolven. China has also been suggested as golf's birthplace.

To sum it up
- Put the most important parts into a few words.
- Don't include details that aren't very important.

Check two sentences that you could use to summarize this text.

_____ a. Many people say that golf was invented in Scotland, but there is no firm proof.

_____ b. In Holland, the game was called kolven.

_____ c. Rome, Holland, Denmark, and China have also been suggested as golf's birthplace.

_____ d. The game kolven was played hundreds of years ago.

Try It

Read this writer profile and think about how to sum it up.

Ferber's First Best-Seller

Author Edna Ferber never expected her book *So Big* to succeed. The book tells the story of a widow who struggles to raise her son alone. Ferber worried that no one would want to buy this book because of its subject and tone. Yet the book sold more than 300,000 copies and won the Pulitzer Prize.

© Hulton Archive

Check the sentence that best summarizes "Ferber's First Best-Seller."

_____ a. Edna Ferber wrote a book about a woman who struggles to raise her son alone. She called it *So Big*.

_____ b. Edna Ferber was surprised by the success of *So Big*, which tells the story of a woman raising her son alone.

_____ c. Edna Ferber won a major prize for her book *So Big*.

Use It

Read this part of a history text. Think about how you would sum it up.

State Nicknames _____

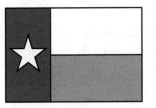

Texas: The Lone Star State

    All states in the U.S. have official state symbols. These symbols include state nicknames. For example, Maine is called "the Pine Tree State," New Hampshire "the Granite State," and Texas "the Lone Star State." California has been "the Golden State" since the Gold Rush of 1849. Two states share a nickname: both Florida and South Dakota are called "the Sunshine State."

Check the sentence that best summarizes the text.

_____ a. Two states share a nickname.

_____ b. The state of Florida has a nickname.

_____ c. Every state has official symbols, including state nicknames.

_____ d. Texas is sometimes called "the Lone Star State."

_____ e. California has been called "the Golden State" since 1849.

Putting It in Other Words

◆ *Paraphrasing*

As you read, think about what the writer says. Think about other ways to say it. Putting ideas in other words will help you understand them. It will help you recall them, too.

This Is the Idea

Read this part of a history text. Put the ideas in other words.

> # The Stanley Steamers
>
> In the early days of the automobile, the Stanley brothers built and sold cars powered by steam engines. Unlike early gasoline engines, steam engines weren't noisy, didn't shake and rattle, and had more get-up-and-go. However, most people found them hard to drive.

You could put the pros and cons of steam engines in these other words: "Steam engines were quiet, smooth, and powerful, but they weren't easy to drive."

Take a Closer Look

To put it in other words

- Think about what it means.
- Look away from the text.
- Imagine telling someone what it says.

Read this part of an art text. Put the ideas in other words.

> Use a magnifying glass to look at a black-and-white photograph in a newspaper. You will see that the grays are actually tiny black dots. That's because a news photograph is photographed again through a screen. The screen breaks the image up into tiny dots of different sizes. From a distance, these dots blend into one another. They make the grays that we think we see.

Circle the sentence that puts the text in blue ink into other words.

a. When we look at the dots from far away, they blur together. They seem to be shades of gray.

b. Pictures in a newspaper are actually made of tiny dots. You can see them if you look at the pictures through a magnifying glass.

Try It

Read this part of a science text. Put the ideas in other words.

This Plant Eats Meat

Plants use nitrogen when they turn sunlight into food. Most plants get the nitrogen they need from the soil. However, the Venus flytrap gets nitrogen by eating insects. When an insect lands on one of the flytrap's hinged leaves, the leaf snaps shut, trapping the insect. In five to ten days, the plant digests the insect.

Here are two ways that readers might put the next-to-last sentence in "This Plant Eats Meat" into other words. Circle the better one.

a. If an insect settles on a leaf, the two parts of the leaf clamp together quickly. The insect is caught.

b. An insect might get caught if it settles on a leaf because the leaf has a hinge. The plant gets nitrogen.

Use It

Read this part of a business text. Put the ideas in other words.

How Money Works

Suppose that there was no money. A farmer who needed a new truck would have to find a truck dealer who would take vegetables for payment. A barber who wanted vegetables would have to find a farmer who needed a haircut. Money takes the place of direct trades like those. The farmer, truck dealer, and barber are all willing to sell their goods and services for money. Then they use that money to buy the goods and services they need.

1. Complete the sentence to describe a direct trade in other words.
   A doctor who wanted a haircut would have to _____

   _____

2. Complete the sentence to tell the writer's point in other words.
   We use money instead of _____

   _____

Deciding What It's About

◆ *Recognizing the Topic*

Most news reports are about one topic. Most charts, ads, and articles are about one topic. Sometimes the topic is spelled out for you. At other times, you will have to figure out the topic.

This Is the Idea

Look at this brochure and decide what it is about.

> # Which Computer Is Right for You?
>
> ### Desktop Models
> - may have larger screens
> - usually cost less
> - don't break as often
>
> ### Laptop Models
> - travel with you
> - take up less space
> - may use less power

The words in blue ink help you know that the topic of this brochure is desktop and laptop computers. The title tells you that it will be about computers. The column headings tell you that one column is about desktop computers and the other about laptop computers.

Take a Closer Look

To decide what the topic is, look at
- a title
- a picture
- a headline or headings
- repeated words on one topic

Look at this instruction sheet. Decide what it is about.

> ### Before You Order Shades
>
> Decide whether you will mount your shades inside or outside the window frames. Then measure the width of your window in three places. Measure across the top, at the middle, and at the bottom. For shades mounted inside, use the smallest of the three measurements. For shades mounted outside, use the largest.

Write your answers.

1. When should you follow these directions?

   _____

2. What is the topic of these directions?

   _____

Try It

Read this paragraph from a book. Decide what it is about.

──── Shopping for a Bird ────

The type of chicken you choose should be determined by how you plan to cook it. If you will broil or fry it, get a young bird weighing about three pounds. If you want to roast it, get a larger bird, perhaps weighing six pounds. If you plan to make chicken stew, look for older birds, which have more flavor.

Write your answers.

1. Judging from the title alone, could this be about buying a pet?

   _____

2. Judging from the picture alone, does this seem to be about pets?

   _____

3. What is the topic of the paragraph?

   _____

Use It

Read the title and look at the picture. Then read the paragraph.

A "Must-See" in Washington, D.C.

An Act of Congress founded the National Portrait Gallery in 1962. This gallery owns about 4,500 portraits of men and women. These people have all added something to the history or life of this country. Subjects include Native Americans, Presidents, artists, and writers.

National Portrait Gallery, Smithsonian Institution

Write your answers.

1. Judging from the title alone, could this be about a park?

   _____

2. Judging from the title *and* the picture, what is this likely to be about?

   _____

3. What is the topic of the paragraph?

   _____

Using the Topic

◆ *Anchoring Understanding on the Topic*

First, decide what the topic of the writing is. (See Lesson 8.) Keep the topic in mind as you read. Focus your attention on what is most important to the topic.

This Is the Idea

Which parts of this post office brochure are most important to the topic?

> # Getting Mail after a Move
>
> Are you moving to a new home? You certainly want your mail to be sent there, but that won't happen automatically. You must tell the post office that you're moving. Ask for a change-of-address form and fill it out. It's simple and easy to do. Your old post office will forward your first-class mail for a year.

The title says that the brochure will tell you how to get mail after a move. The parts in blue ink are most important to this topic, and the other parts are less important.

Take a Closer Look

As you read, ask yourself

- Is this about the topic?
- Is this really important to the topic, or is it something that I don't need to remember?

Which parts of this article are most important to the topic?

> # Photographing Animals
>
> People love to have pictures of their pets, but some people say that it's easier to photograph squirming children! The trick to getting pets to stay still is feeding them. Some animals are more relaxed with their owners present. Others are calmer with the owners away.
>
>

This is one statement that is important to someone who wants to photograph pets: "Some animals are more relaxed with their owners present." Write another important statement from the reading.

_____

_____

Try It

Which parts of this consumer tip are most important to the topic?

★ ★ ★ ★ ★ ★ **A Tip for Smart Shoppers** ★ ★ ★ ★ ★ ★

Food items are sold in packages of many sizes. They're printed in bright colors to catch your eye. The prices on the packages may vary widely. To compare the true costs of the foods, don't look only at the package price. Instead, compare the cost per ounce and the cost per portion. The unit-pricing label will help.

	UNIT PRICE	YOU PAY
07789012288 DD	64.5¢	
03/06/02	PER QUART	**$2.58**
02-20-20 012238		
2% LOWFAT MILK 1 GL.		

Write your answers. The first one is done for you.

1. What is the topic?

   how to compare the true costs of foods

2. Write one statement that is important to the topic.

   _____

   _____

Use It

Which parts of this civics text are most important to the topic?

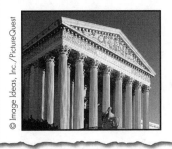
© Image Ideas, Inc./PictureQuest

The Highest Court in the Land

Courts decide questions of law. Towns and cities have courts, and states have courts, too. The United States Supreme Court is the highest court in the country. It is made up of one Chief Justice and eight associate justices. They hear cases in Washington, D.C. The Supreme Court tries only cases that affect the laws of the nation as a whole.

Write your answers.

1. What is the topic?

   _____

2. Write two statements that are important to the topic.

   _____

   _____

   _____

   _____

Finding the Writer's Point

◆ *Recognizing the Main Idea*

Writers sometimes state their point in a sentence, but sometimes they don't state it. Even if a writer does not state the point, you can often figure it out. It is a statement about the topic.

This Is the Idea

Read this part of a science text, and look for the writer's point.

Rods and Cones

In the eye are two kinds of nerve cells, called rods and cones, that react to light. Rods and cones work together, the strengths of one balancing the weaknesses of the other. The rods see better in dim light, but they can't see color. The cones see colors well, but they see best in bright light.

The writer tells you what rods and cones are and then makes an important point about them. That point is the sentence in blue ink. It is the main idea of this part of the article.

Take a Closer Look

Read this science text and look for the writer's main point.

The inclined plane is a simple machine that makes work easier. A plane is a flat surface, like a board, plank, or ramp. Pushing a heavy box up a ramp and into the back of a truck is much easier than lifting it up into the truck. The ramp is an inclined plane, a simple machine that makes work easier.

To find the writer's point

- Look for a general statement about the topic, especially in the first or last sentence.
- Read all the sentences and decide what the writer wants to say about the topic.

Circle your answer.

1. What is this article about?
   a. a heavy box   b. the inclined plane

Write your answer.

2. Which sentence states the writer's point?

_____

Try It

As you read this health brochure, look for the writer's point.

What Pollen Does to People

Most plants produce tiny grains called pollen as part of the process of making fertile seeds. These tiny pollen grains shake loose from the plant and drift on the wind. People breathe air with pollen grains in it, but the grains are so small many people don't notice. Not everyone is so lucky, however. Pollen makes many people sneeze.

Circle your answer.

1. What is the topic of this health brochure? *Hint:* Look at the title.
   a. how plants make fertile seeds   b. how pollen affects people

Write your answer.

2. Which sentence states the writer's point? *Hint:* It's a statement about the topic.

_____

Use It

As you read this part of a history text, look for the writer's point.

© Corbis

Susan B. Anthony and Women's Right to Vote

When Susan B. Anthony began her work for women's rights, women could not vote. To show how strongly she felt that they should have the right to vote, she voted herself. She was fined for it. Until her death in 1906, she worked for the right of women to vote. In 1920, the United States gave women the vote. In the end, Anthony won her struggle for women's rights, though she wasn't alive to see it.

Which sentence states the writer's point? Write your answer.

_____

_____

Using the Writer's Point

♦ *Building on the Main Idea*

First, decide what the writer's point is. (See Lesson 10.) Keep the writer's point in mind as you read. Use the point to check your understanding and to help you remember the important parts of what you read.

This Is the Idea

Read this job-hunting advice and think about the writer's point.

> When you're looking for a job, be sure to highlight all the skills you have to offer. As a first step, take a survey of your skills. For one week, keep track of everything you do at work, at home, in school, or in a hobby. At the end of the week, classify these activities by skill. Don't exaggerate your skills, but don't overlook any, either.

The writer makes the point that you should be sure not to overlook any skills that you have to offer. That point suggests that you should look beyond the obvious skills that you use at work. You can extend the writer's point. Before an interview, you can think about your skills and remind yourself to mention any that relate to the job.

Take a Closer Look

Read this parenting advice and think about the writer's point.

Teaching Your Pre-schooler to Share

Children are more likely to succeed in school if they learn to share at home first. **In school, a child is asked to share many things, from crayons to the teacher's attention. If the child has to learn to share in school, it can get in the way of other lessons to be learned.**

As you read, ask yourself

- What is important about the writer's point?
- How can I help myself remember the point?
- How can I use the point?

The writer's point is in blue ink. Based on that point, what would be a good way to prepare pre-schoolers for starting school? Circle your answer.

a. Give each child a sandwich for lunch so that they don't fight.
b. Put pieces of sandwich on a platter for the children to share.
c. Let the children have whatever they want for lunch.

Try It

Read this civics text and think about the writer's point.

How Laws Are Made

Congress, the President, and the Supreme Court all play parts in deciding what our laws will be. U.S. laws begin as bills written and passed in Congress. In most cases, the President must approve a bill before it becomes law. Even then, the Supreme Court may decide the law conflicts with the U.S. Constitution. Then the law must be changed.

1. Which statement agrees with the writer's point? Circle your answer.
   a. Congress, the President, and the Supreme Court are all involved in making and approving our laws.
   b. The President can act alone to make our laws and does not have to work with Congress or the Supreme Court.

2. Which statement is implied by the writer's point? Circle your answer.
   a. The Supreme Court can make a new law.
   b. The Supreme Court cannot make a new law.

Use It

Read this advice and think about the writer's point.

Cut It Down to Size

Big jobs can seem overwhelming. But remember that a journey of a thousand miles begins with a single step. Break a big job into many small steps. Spend some time thinking about the job and its many parts. Then break it into parts that make sense. Schedule a small step for each day or hour until the job is done.

Circle your answer.

1. Which statement agrees with the writer's point?
   a. It's best to take on a big job all at once to get it over with.
   b. Big jobs are easier if you do them a little bit at a time.

Write your answer.

2. Write two small steps that are part of painting the walls in a room.

   _____

   _____

Finding Useful Details

♦ *Recognizing Significant Details*

Details are the
little things in
apiece of writing.
Some details are
useful because they
help you understand
the writer's point.
Other details may
beinteresting but
not important to
the point.

This Is the Idea

Which details are most useful in getting the point of this consumer tip?

Comparing Phone Cards

Prepaid phone cards are useful when you travel. You can buy them at many stores. **Compare several cards before you buy one.** Two cards may differ in cost and offer different numbers of minutes. To compare, check the cost per minute. Just divide the card's total price by the number of minutes.

The writer's point is in **bold type**. The sentences in blue ink state important details about this idea. They help you understand why and how to compare cards. The first two sentences are not as important.

Take a Closer Look

**As you read,
ask yourself**

- Is this detail useful or is it just interesting?
- Does this detail help me understand the writer's point?

Which details help you understand days named for Odin or his family?

Names of the Days

Odin was the leader of the gods in Norse myth. Four days of the week are named for him or his family. Tuesday is named for his son, Tiw. Tiw was a war god that had one hand. Wednesday is named for Odin himself (who was also called Woden). Thursday is named for Odin's son Thor. And many people believe Friday is named for Odin's wife, Frigga.

Check each detail that helps you understand specific days of the week named for Odin or his family.

_____ a. Odin was the leader of the gods in Norse myth.

_____ b. Tuesday is named for Tiw, Odin's son.

_____ c. Tiw was a war god that had one hand.

_____ d. Wednesday is named for Odin himself.

Try It

Which details help you understand the writer's point?

Beating Egg Whites

Beaten egg whites make dishes light and airy, but they can be hard to prepare. First, be sure the whites contain no yolk. Yolks can ruin the texture. Eggs at room temperature work better than icy ones. Beat egg whites in a clean, deep bowl, and use them at once. The results will delight you.

© Image Source/elektraVision/
PictureQuest

List three details that are important to understanding the right way to beat egg whites.

1. _____

2. _____

3. _____

Use It

Which details help you understand the writer's point?

The Pledge of Allegiance

Many Americans know the Pledge of Allegiance. They say it in schools and at many events. This pledge has an interesting history. It was not written by the country's leaders. It was written for a children's magazine. The author, Francis Bellamy, thought it would be spoken just once, on Columbus Day. Teachers and students liked the verse, though, and kept using it. At first they said it once a year. Then they started saying it every day. The first version was slightly shorter. Two small changes were made over time.

List three details that help you understand the interesting history of the Pledge of Allegiance.

1. _____

2. _____

3. _____

Using Details

◆ *Understanding the Significance of Details*

Some details are more important than others. Some details help you do or understand something, while others help you make a choice. Look for useful details.

This Is the Idea

Which details in this post office brochure help you address an envelope?

Write the Complete Address

You want the mail that you send to arrive, so write the complete mailing address. For example, a city might have both Hill Road and Hill Court, so write "Rd." or "Ct.," not "Hill" alone. Include apartment numbers, as well as the city, state, and zip code. A post office clerk can help you find the zip code.

You want to know what the post office means by a complete address. The details in blue ink explain what is meant by this. The other details might be interesting, but they don't tell you what you want to know.

Take a Closer Look

Which details in this science text help you tell how far away a storm is?

As you read, ask yourself

- What makes this detail useful?
- Will this detail help me do or understand something?
- Will this detail help me make a choice?

Where's That Storm?_____

Lightning heats air molecules to create thunder. Light moves faster than sound, however, so we see lightning before we hear thunder. You can use this fact to estimate how far away a storm is. Count the seconds between lightning and thunder. If it's 5 seconds, the storm is about a mile away. If it's 10 seconds, the storm is two miles away, and so on. And if you see lightning and hear thunder at the same time, the storm is right overhead.

Check two details that help you figure out how far away a storm is.

_____ a. Lightning heats air molecules to create thunder.

_____ b. Light moves faster than sound, however.

_____ c. Count the seconds between lightning and thunder.

_____ d. If it's 5 seconds, the storm is about a mile away.

Try It

Which details help you decide what to tell a child about dangers online?

Keep Your Kids Safe Online

Many sites on the Internet are good for children. But kids need to learn to stay safe online. For instance, it can be dangerous to use their real names on the Internet. So give your kids some clear safety guidelines. It's also important not to tell anyone where they live or go to school. And they should never meet an online friend without permission.

Using the details in the reading, write three safety rules for children who go online.

1. Don't _____

2. Don't _____

3. Don't _____

Use It

Which details help you see how George Eastman changed photography?

George Eastman

Early cameras were large and hard to use. Few people took pictures. Cameras used large, clumsy plates, not film. George Eastman replaced the plates with film. Then he created a small, simple camera that held the film. Now someone could take pictures by just pressing a button. In a few years, his cameras were selling by the thousands.

© Hulton Archive

Write your answers.

1. Why did few people use cameras at first?

   _____

2. What did Eastman's camera let people do?

   _____

3. What detail helps you conclude that taking pictures became popular?

   _____

Deciding When It Happens

◆ *Following a Sequence*

Most reports of events, travel articles, and history articles list events in the same order they happened. Most directions list steps in the order you should follow.

This Is the Idea

Here is part of a travel article. As you read it, notice the order of events.

> The short flight from Pittsburgh to New York offers great views. Your first glimpse of the city is the Statue of Liberty. You fly right over her! Then you turn and fly north, directly over Manhattan. You're so low that you feel you could touch the skyscrapers. Finally, you turn lazily toward the airport.

Here are three events listed out of order. They're numbered to show the right order. Notice that the numbering matches the order in the text.

2 You fly north, over Manhattan.

3 You turn toward the airport.

1 You glimpse the Statue of Liberty.

Take a Closer Look

What shows the order of events?

- the order in the text
- words that refer to time, such as *after, again, as soon as, at last, before, finally, first, later, next, now, second, start, then, when,* and *while*

As you read this history text, notice the order of the events.

> The Liberty Bell was cast in London and then shipped to Philadelphia. It arrived there in August of 1752. In September of that year, it cracked while it was being tested. In 1777, the bell was removed and hidden so that the British army wouldn't get it. In 1778, it returned to Philadelphia. It now hangs there near Independence Hall.

Which of these events happened *second?* Circle your answer. ***Hint:*** Find each event in the article.

a. The bell cracked.

b. The bell was shipped.

c. The bell was returned.

d. The bell was hidden.

Try It

As you read this explanation, notice the order of the steps.

How Smoke Detectors Work

One kind of smoke detector uses a photocell to "see" the smoke. When the detector is turned on, a tiny light shines on the photocell. When a fire starts, smoke enters the detector, and it dims the light. The photocell detects the change and closes a switch. That makes the alarm sound.

Number the following steps to show the order in which they occur.

_____ Light shines on the photocell.

_____ Smoke dims the light.

_____ The photocell detects the change in light.

_____ Smoke enters the detector.

Use It

As you read these directions, notice the order of the steps.

How to Install Your New Smoke Detector

First, mount the base plate on the wall six inches below the ceiling. Next, snap the battery into its holder. Press the clip onto the connectors at the top of the battery. Place the cover on the base plate. Then press it until it snaps into place. Finally, push the TEST button. A beep will show that the alarm is working.

Circle your answers.

1. Which of these two steps should you do first?
   a. snap battery into holder   b. press clip onto connectors

2. Which of these two steps should you do first?
   a. mount base plate   b. put cover on

Write your answer.

3. If the cover is loose, what step did you probably skip?

_____

Using Time Order

Notice the order of steps or events and think about why they happen in that order. Think about what would happen if the order were different, and think about what is likely to happen next.

This Is the Idea

Read this memo and think about why timing is important in it.

To the Building Staff

A tenant has complained about a missing package. Please be sure to follow the established procedures. When a package arrives, list it in the package log book. Then buzz the tenant to announce that a package has arrived. If the package cannot be delivered, put it in the secure closet.

The order of the steps is important. Suppose that a package arrives when you are on duty. You put it into the closet without listing it in the log book. The next person on duty won't know that the package arrived.

As you read, ask yourself

- Why are the steps in this order?
- Why did the events happen in this order?
- What would happen if the order changed?
- What will probably happen next?

Take a Closer Look

Read this cooking tip and think about why timing is important in it.

The Secret of a Perfect Stir-Fry

If you cook mushrooms too long, you'll know why their name starts with "mush." But undercooked celery will be as crunchy as raw celery. In general, hard vegetables like carrots and onions need more cooking than soft ones like leafy greens. Add things that need more cooking earlier than things that need less.

Write your answers about cooking a stir-fry meal.

1. If you add onions before bean sprouts, which will cook longer?

_____

2. If you add onions at the very end, will they be soft or crunchy?

_____

Try It

Read this part of an article and think about the order of events.

Installing an Extension Phone

Do you need another phone in another room? You can save money by installing it yourself. First, decide where you want the new phone outlet to be. Then measure for the wire you will need to connect the new outlet to the nearest old one. Measure every bend and turn. After you buy the wire, unroll it along the wall to make sure that you have enough.

What might go wrong if you bought the wire before deciding where you wanted to put the new phone outlet? Write your answer.

_____

_____

Use It

Read this science text and think about why timing is important in it.

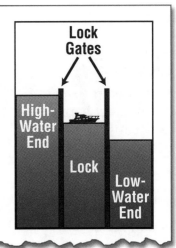

Locks allow ships to sail between two sections of a canal with different water levels. A lock is a small part of the canal with watertight gates at each end. Workers can raise or lower the lock's water level by using valves. Suppose a ship approaches the lock from the high-water end. First, workers make sure that the level in the lock matches the high-water level. Then they open the gates at the high end, and the ship enters the lock. The gates are closed, and workers open valves to let water out of the lock. When the level in the lock matches the low-water level, they open the gates at the low end. Then the ship sails through onto the lower section of the canal.

Write your answers.

1. What might happen if workers didn't check the water level before they opened a lock gate?

_____

2. What would happen if both lock gates were open at the same time?

_____

Deciding Why It Happens

◆ *Recognizing Cause and Effect*

To find a cause, ask, "Why did this happen? What was the reason for it?" To find an effect, ask, "What is the result of what happened?" Look for words and patterns that signal causes and effects.

This Is the Idea

As you read this business advice, look for causes and effects.

Take a Stand Against Long Meetings

If you're tired of meetings that drag on, take the chairs out of the meeting room or hold meetings in a room without chairs. People don't linger if they have to stand. Because they are a little uncomfortable, they say what they need to say and don't discuss unimportant things.

What will happen if people have to stand? They won't linger. Why will they say what they need to say and skip the unimportant things? Because they are a little uncomfortable.

Take a Closer Look

As you read this parenting advice, look for causes and effects.

Never Leave a Child or Pet in a Parked Car

Sunlight comes through the window of the car easily because glass lets light through it. In the car, dark surfaces absorb the sunlight, so they are warmed by it. They radiate heat, but that heat can't escape from the car, since glass doesn't let radiant heat through it. The car gets hotter and hotter.

Look for

- *because* or *since*: An effect happens because a cause happens.
- *if . . . then*: If a cause happens, then an effect happens.
- *so:* A cause happens, so an effect happens.
- *as a result:* An effect happens as a result of a cause.

Write your answers. The first one is done for you.

1. Why is sunlight able to enter the car?

   <u>because the window glass lets light pass through it</u>

2. Why doesn't the radiant heat go out of the car as sunlight came in?

   _____

Try It

Read this troubleshooting flow chart and think about causes and effects.

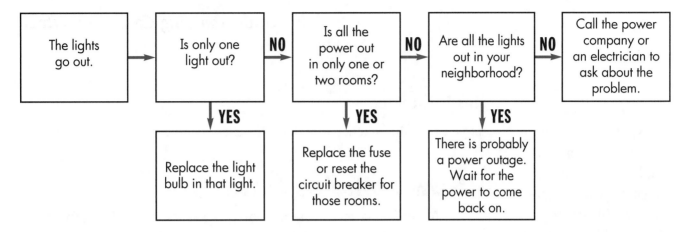

| The lights go out. | → | Is only one light out? | **NO** → | Is all the power out in only one or two rooms? | **NO** → | Are all the lights out in your neighborhood? | **NO** → | Call the power company or an electrician to ask about the problem. |

↓ **YES** Replace the light bulb in that light.

↓ **YES** Replace the fuse or reset the circuit breaker for those rooms.

↓ **YES** There is probably a power outage. Wait for the power to come back on.

Write your answers.

1. What is the likely cause if only one light is out?

   _____

2. What is the likely cause if all the power is out in only one or two rooms?

   _____

Use It

As you read this parenting advice, look for causes and effects.

Many children resist learning math because they can't see that it will do them any good in the real world. You can help change that attitude at home. Your child will see the value of math if you invite your child to help, or at least to watch, when you have practical math work to do. That might include paying bills or figuring the cost of a loan.

Write your answers.

1. Why do some kids not want to learn math?

   _____

2. What can you do to show your child that math is useful?

   _____

   _____

Using Reasons

◆ *Understanding Cause and Effect*

As you read, look for causes that make something happen and effects that result from causes. Use causes and effects to check your understanding, to help you summarize, and to predict outcomes.

This Is the Idea

As you read this science text, look for causes and effects.

How Potholes Form

A pothole can begin forming in the winter when water under the pavement freezes. Water expands when it freezes, so the ice heaves upward, breaking a piece out of the pavement. In the spring, the ice melts, and the broken piece sinks back into a muddy hole.

The text explains how potholes form. To check your understanding, you could ask yourself what causes potholes to appear in the spring. To use the information in the article, you could predict that you should watch out for potholes as the weather gets warmer.

Take a Closer Look

As you read, ask yourself

- Why did that happen? What made it happen? What caused it?
- What resulted from that?
- What other results might there be?

As you read this health brochure, look for causes and effects.

Meat and poultry can make you and your family ill if you don't cook them right. The greatest danger comes from bacteria. These are tiny creatures that live in raw meat and can cause disease. If you cook meat fully, you will kill them. If you eat raw or rare meat, they may still be living in it.

Write your answers.

1. Why should you cook chicken until it's completely done?

_____

2. What might happen if juices from raw chicken got onto a roll?

_____

Try It

As you read this part of a science text, look for causes and effects.

If you have a comb in your pocket, you can chirp like a cricket. Just run your fingernail along the teeth. Under each of their front wings, male crickets have a row of teeth like those on your comb. To make a chirp, they very quickly rub the top of one wing along the teeth on the other. Only male crickets chirp, and they do it mainly to attract female crickets.

Write your answers.

1. What results from a cricket's rubbing one wing against another?

_____

2. Why do crickets chirp?

_____

Use It

As you read this part of a science text, look for causes and effects.

Your body processes food to get energy to be active. Calories measure how much energy a food contains or how much an activity burns. If you consume and burn off the same number of calories, you'll stay the same weight. If you eat more than you burn, your body stores the extra energy as fat—and you gain weight. About 3,500 extra calories equals a pound of fat.

1. Based on the reading, what would be the best way to lose weight?

_____

2. Many doctors suggest that to lose weight, you eat 1,000 calories less than you burn every day. If you followed this advice, about how much weight would you lose in a week?

_____

Finding Groups

Classifying is putting things in groups. Writers usually group things because the things are alike in some way. Notice how the members of a group are alike. Think about other things that might fit in the group.

This Is the Idea

As you read this city budget chart, notice how expenses are grouped.

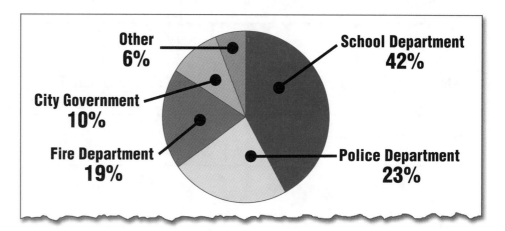

Each wedge includes many expenses. For example, the fire department budget includes pay, trucks, repair of fire stations, health care, and uniforms. If all of those things were listed separately, the chart would be very hard to read. Grouping makes it simpler and clearer.

Take a Closer Look

As you read this sales brochure, notice how materials are grouped.

Your Kitchen Floor

You can choose from many kinds of flooring. Vinyl flooring "gives" a bit, so it's easy on your legs and the dishes you drop. Wood is handsome, but it's sure to stain with time. Tile is sturdy, but it may be slippery when wet. All of these come in many styles and a wide range of prices.

What might make you decide against wide pine boards as the flooring for your new kitchen? Write your answer. ***Hint:*** First decide what group the flooring belongs in.

Try It

Read this course listing. Notice how students are grouped.

Practical Math:
Basic math you need to know for everyday use.

Business Math:
Math for people who are planning to start their own businesses.

Tax Math:
Math for calculating your estimated taxes and completing your tax return.

You're thinking of opening a shop where you will sell shoes and hand-bags. Which course would suit you? Write your answer.

_____

Use It

Read this part of a single taxpayer's rate chart. Look for groups.

If Taxpayer's Income Is		Then Estimated Taxes Are		
Above	But Not Over	Base Tax	+ Rate	Of the Amount Over
$0	$6,000	$0.00	10%	$0
$6,000	$26,250	$600.00	15%	$6,000
$26,250	$63,550	$3,637.50	27%	$26,250
$63,550	$132,600	$13,708.50	30%	$63,550

Write your answers.

1. If Reth's income is $17,500, what is his base tax?

_____

2. If Drina's income is $4,500, what is her base tax?

_____

3. If Hana's income is $28,100, what is her rate above the base tax?

_____

Using Groups

♦ *Understanding Classification*

This Is the Idea

Read this small print from an airline ad. Think about groups.

Restrictions

Discount fares apply only for travel on EastWest Airlines and NorthSouth Airlines. Round-trip travel must begin after April 10 and end before June 10. Trips must include a Saturday night stay. Discounts do not apply to children under 12 traveling alone.

To get a discount, a person has to fit into several groups. A 30-year-old who will travel on EastWest Airlines between May 9 and May 18 will get a discount. A 10-year-old traveling alone on the same airline at the same time will not get a discount.

Take a Closer Look

As you read,
ask yourself

- Why did the writer put things in groups?
- What do the groups mean to me?

As you read this part of a news story, notice how jobs are grouped.

Where the Jobs Will Be

Experts are predicting that most new jobs will be in the hotel and restaurant industries. Jobs in technology, including computer makers, will be the next largest group. Third will be jobs in health care. The slowest growth will be in auto manufacturing.

If you were planning to take a job training course, what type of study would give you the best chance at a job? Write your answer. *Hint:* Decide which group you would belong in.

Try It

Read this chart. Why does it put kinds of pets in groups?

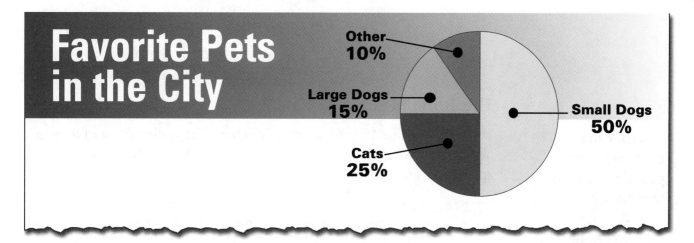

If you were going to open a pet shop in this city, would it make more sense to sell tiny pug dogs or huge Great Danes? Write your answer.

_____

Use It

Read this contents list from a manual and think about the groups in it.

Problems and Solutions

Setup Problems
    If you're having trouble getting started, see Chapter 1.
Printing Problems
    If your printer is set up but won't work, see Chapter 2.
Ink Problems
    If pages don't look the way they should, see Chapter 3.
Paper Problems
    If paper does not feed as it should, see Chapter 4.

Write your answers.

1. If you can't figure out how to connect the printer to your computer, which chapter should you turn to?

_____

2. If pages are coming out dark and blurry, which chapter should you turn to?

_____

Finding Like and Unlike

◆ *Recognizing Comparison and Contrast*

A writer may compare things, pointing out ways that they are alike. A writer may contrast things, pointing out ways that they are different.

This Is the Idea

Terry has been looking for a new apartment. She made this chart to help her decide which one to choose. Read Terry's chart. Notice how the apartments are alike and different.

	BRs	Baths	DR	AC	Notes
19th St.	1	1	yes	no	elevator building
2nd Ave.	2	1	no	yes	walkup
12th St.	2	2	no	no	elevator building
38th St.	1	1	no	yes	walkup

The chart helps Terry compare and contrast the apartments. In each column, she can see specific ways that they are alike or different.

Take a Closer Look

Words used to compare

- the words *also, both, like,* and *same*

Words used to contrast

- words that end in *er,* such as *wider*
- the words *but, however, in contrast, though, while,* and *unlike*

Read this article. Decide how the old and new museums are different.

New Museum Opens

The new city art museum is a great improvement over the old one. The new museum is larger and brighter. It is much easier to get to because it's right at a major subway stop. It doesn't have the charm that the old building had. However, the paintings are just as beautiful as always.

Write three things that make the new museum different from the old one.

1. _____

2. _____

3. _____

Try It

Read these ads and decide how the cars are alike and different.

Hear the Grizzly Roar

You'll love the thrill of driving the new Grizzly V-8. Its engine throbs with power, eager to take you where you want to go. The Grizzly is a solid, roomy car, just right for the big family.

Take a Sparkle For A Spin

The new Sparkle is kind to your wallet. Its new hybrid engine uses little gas and doesn't pollute much. The Sparkle is light and nimble, perfect for the young at heart.

Circle your answers.

1. Which ad stresses power rather than savings?
   a. the Grizzly ad   b. the Sparkle ad

2. Which car is probably smaller?
   a. the Grizzly   b. the Sparkle

Use It

Read this chart and decide how the foods are alike and different.

Breakfast Cereal (per two-ounce serving)			
	Fat	Carbohydrate	Protein
Snappies	13 grams	31 grams	5 grams
Fizzles	20 grams	42 grams	2 grams
Poppers	6 grams	22 grams	9 grams

Write your answers.

1. Which cereal has the least fat?

_____

2. Which cereal has the least carbohydrate?

_____

3. Which cereal has the most protein?

_____

Using What You Find

♦ *Understanding Comparison and Contrast*

This Is the Idea

Read this painting advice. Why are likenesses and differences important?

Suit the Paint to the Site

If you're planning to repaint, choose the type of paint that suits the room. In rooms where walls are likely to need washing, such as kitchens, use a semi-gloss paint. In living rooms, a flat paint is a better choice. It won't wipe clean with a swipe of a sponge, but it reflects light more softly.

The advice points out important differences between two types of paint. These differences will be important if you're planning to repaint your kitchen or living room. The writer doesn't discuss bathrooms and bedrooms, but you can tell which paint would be better for those rooms.

Take a Closer Look

Think about

- what makes things alike or different
- what you can say about the likenesses and differences in general
- why the likenesses and differences are important
- what they suggest that isn't said

Why are likenesses and differences important in this ad?

We've Got Two Great Calling Plans!

PLAN 1 $19.99 monthly	**PLAN 2 $39.99 monthly**
• unlimited weekend calling	• unlimited weekend calling
• 100 weekday minutes	• 400 weekday minutes
• extra minutes 30 cents each	• extra minutes 10 cents each

Write your answers.

1. You don't make many calls during the week. Which plan is better for you?

   _____

2. You use your phone for business. Which plan is better for you?

   _____

Try It

Read this game review. Why are differences important?

—Two Games for Kids—

Kids of all ages seem to love the TV cartoon character Bob the Busy Bee. Now there are two games based on the character. "Bob Counts" teaches counting and basic number skills. "Bob Saves the Day" is an action game in which Bob has to escape from dragons and "evil masters of space."

Write your answers.

1. Which game seems better for Lisa, who will start kindergarten next year?

   _____

2. Which game seems likely to include violence and scary pictures?

   _____

Use It

Why are likenesses and differences important in this sales brochure?

Choosing a Fence

If you are choosing a fence to dress up your home or business, the choice depends on looks and price. However, if you are choosing a fence for security, looks are less important than strength. A split-rail fence is handsome and doesn't cost much, but it won't keep anyone out. A chain-link fence isn't attractive, but it is solid and secure. The fence around a swimming pool is a special case. The most important purpose is to keep children from falling into the pool, but the fence should look good, too. A stockade fence may be a good choice.

Write your answers.

1. Why would someone choose a split-rail fence over chain-link?

   _____

2. You have a small auto-repair business and want to be sure that it's locked up tight at night. What kind of fence would be good for you?

   _____

Guessing What Will Happen

◆ *Predicting Outcomes*

As you read, think about what is likely to happen as time passes. Predict what will happen. Use what you know and any hints that the writer may give you.

This Is the Idea

Read this advice to predict what will happen as you cook pasta.

Pasta Perfect

Pasta absorbs water as it cooks and softens, so you should always use a large, deep pot and plenty of water. Bring the water to an active, rolling boil, not just a gentle simmer. The best pasta is cooked so that it's still firm when you bite a piece. Lift a piece from the boiling water, cool it, and bite it. When it's cooked but still firm, it's done.

From the fact in blue ink, you can predict that pasta will get thicker and softer as it cooks. You can also predict that using too little water will mean that the pasta can't cook properly.

Take a Closer Look

These help you guess what will happen:
- a pattern of events
- the writer's point and conclusions
- causes and effects
- what you know

Read this advice to predict what will happen as you use the calendar.

Teaching a Child to Plan

Most children do not have a good sense of time. As a result, planning is hard for them. You can help them learn to plan by marking events and obligations on a calendar. For example, suppose your child has a school report due in a week. You could mark days for doing research, writing a first draft, correcting the draft, and making the final copy.

What will happen if your child follows planned steps to prepare a school report? Write your answer.

_____

Try It

Read this business text. Predict what will happen if you overcharge.

Setting Prices

If you own a small shop, you have to decide how much to charge for the things you sell. Often, the manufacturer will suggest a price. But you may not be able to charge that much. If other shops charge less, you'll probably have to meet their price in order to attract customers.

Write your answers.

1. What is likely to happen if you charge what the manufacturer suggests, but other shops charge less?

_____

2. What is likely to happen if other shops charge what the manufacturer suggests, but you charge less?

_____

Use It

Read this science text. Predict what will happen to an insect on its own.

© Steve Cole/PhotoDisc/PictureQuest

Insect Colonies

Some insects live in groups, or colonies, in which each member of the group has a job to do. Honey bees live this way, and so do ants. Each honey bee in a hive must do its job if the hive is to succeed. Similarly, each ant must do its job if the ant colony is to succeed. And to survive, each individual insect needs the work of the others in the colony.

1. If a honey bee is stranded away from its hive, what do you predict will happen to the bee?

_____

2. If an accident kills most of the ants in a colony, what do you predict could happen to the colony?

_____

Using Your Prediction

A prediction is a good guess about what may happen as time passes. (See Lesson 22.) Use a prediction to check your understanding and to plan what you should do. Use it to test what the writer says and to test general statements.

This Is the Idea

Read this part of a driver's guide. Think about what you should do.

The Danger of Tailgating

Tailgating is getting too close to the car ahead of you. If you follow too closely, you are asking for trouble. You won't have enough time to react to what the driver in front of you does. What if that car came to a sudden stop? If someone is following you too closely, shift to another lane or pull over and let the tailgater pass you.

You might predict that if you tailgate, you won't have enough time to avoid a crash. And if you don't let a tailgater pass you, you might predict that the car will hit yours if you have to stop suddenly. These predictions can help you decide how you will drive.

Take a Closer Look

You may want to
- stop something from happening
- make sure that something does happen
- check your understanding
- check a general statement

Read this part of a cleaning tip. Think about what will happen.

Cleaning Windows as the Pros Do

Professional window washers use lots of sudsy water, not a spray bottle of window cleaner. They leave the water on the window for a while to soften the dirt, but they don't let it dry. Then they sweep the sudsy water away with a squeegee. Finally, they dry the window with a soft dry towel.

What may happen if the window washer lets the soapy water dry before trying to sweep it away? Circle your answer. *Hint:* Think about the dirt.

a. The dirt will be tougher to remove because it will harden again.

b. The dirt will be easier to remove because it will run downward.

Try It

Read this flyer and think about what you should do to get tickets.

See *Oceans Away* for Free!

We have FREE tickets to this exciting new adventure film! We'll be giving them away to the first 100 people who come to the customer service department at the City Bookstore Café. You must come in person, and there will be one ticket per person only. You must bring identification with you.

Write your answers.

1. Predict what will happen if you call the store and ask them to save a ticket for you.

2. Predict what will happen if you go to the store, wait in line, and ask for two tickets when your turn comes.

Use It

Read this owner's manual and think about what will happen to your tires.

Check Your Tire Pressure

Your tires should be inflated to the right pressure. No tire can hold its air forever. Air leaks out little by little. Looking at the tire won't tell you if the pressure is low until the tire is almost flat, so you have to use a pressure gauge. If the pressure is low, your tire will wear faster, and you will not have good control of your car.

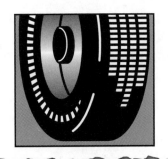

Write your answers.

1. If you drive on a set of tires for a month and then check the pressure, will the pressure be higher or lower than it was at the start?

2. You check your tires every month to make sure the pressure is right. Your neighbor never checks his tires. Whose tires will last longer?

Thinking Clearly

◆ *Drawing Conclusions*

Statements work together. They may be linked by grouping, by cause and effect, or by likenesses and differences. From one statement, you can conclude, or figure out, that another statement makes sense.

This Is the Idea

Read this article. What can you conclude about preventing falls?

Prevent Falls at Home

Many injuries in the home are caused by falls. If you have any trouble with walking, you can prevent falls by lighting passageways, especially stairs, well. Fix loose carpets, rugs, and railings. Add railings and grab bars to tubs. Add them to even the shortest flights of stairs, too.

The article suggests ways that you can prevent falls at home. Read what the article says about loose carpets, rugs, and railings. You can conclude that other forms of loose flooring can be a danger, too. Loose kitchen tiles or floorboards should be repaired as well.

Take a Closer Look

Read this part of a science text. What can you conclude about scientists?

Do Scientists Agree?

For a long time, scientists have debated what killed the dinosaurs that once roamed the Earth. Two scientists suggested that an asteroid struck the Earth, causing great destruction. At first, many other scientists laughed at that idea. Now many scientists accept it.

Remember

- What is true for a group is true for any thing in it.
- If X happened before Y, then Y happened after X.
- If something happens, there must be a reason.
- To make sense, a statement must cover the facts.

What can you conclude? Circle your answer. ***Hint:*** To make sense, a statement must cover the facts.

a. All scientists think alike.

b. Every scientist agrees with every other scientist.

c. Scientists have different ideas about how things happen.

d. A disease of some kind killed the dinosaurs.

Try It

Read this history text. What can you conclude about windmills?

Windmills

At first, human beings used muscle power or animal power to grind grain. The first non-animal power sources were wind and water. Many historians think the earliest windmills were in the Middle East. From there, they spread to Europe and around the world.

© Corbis Images/PictureQuest

Write your answers.

1. Which did people use first, wind, water, or animal power?

   _____

2. Where would the oldest windmills probably be found?

   _____

Use It

Read this article. What can you conclude about your need for sleep?

How Much Sleep Do You Need?

How much sleep do you need? For years, experts have said that all adults need eight hours of sleep. However, a new study has suggested that most people need less than that. One sleep expert said that the important thing to remember is that people are different. She put it this way: "You need as much sleep as you need to feel wide awake and healthy. Let your body tell you how many hours that is."

Write your answers.

1. What can you conclude about sleep experts?

   _____

2. If the new study is right, what can you conclude about how to decide how much sleep you need?

   _____

   _____

Using Clear Thinking

Decide what
you can conclude
from what you read.
(See Lesson 24.)
Use what you
conclude to check
your understanding
or to decide what
you should do.

This Is the Idea

Read this how-to advice. What can you conclude about the paint?

How Much Paint Will You Need?

Follow these steps to decide how much paint you'll need to paint a room. First find the area of the walls by multiplying the lengths of each wall by the height of the room in feet. Subtract the area of the windows and doors. Divide by 350 to decide how many gallons you'll need for each coat.

If you are going to paint a room, you can use this advice to figure out how much paint you should buy. Suppose you find that a small room will need one gallon for each coat. Should you buy only one gallon? From the last sentence, you can conclude that you'll need a second gallon if you want a second coat.

Take a Closer Look

Read about these magazines. What can you conclude about them?

Computer Monthly	Today's Computers
If you're confused by your computer or can't figure out how to use your new software, this is the magazine for you.	We bring you the latest news, the hottest breakthroughs, and cool tips, shortcuts, tricks, and secrets for the power user!

Write your answers.

1. Which would be better for someone just starting to use a computer?

   _____

2. Which would be better for you?

   _____

Try It

Read about armadillos. What can you conclude about them?

Given a choice, armadillos prefer to eat insects. If insects aren't available, they will eat berries. Like prairie dogs, armadillos live in burrows. Their paws and claws are good for digging. In some very dry areas, the ground is as hard as concrete. It's too hard for even armadillos to dig.

© Getty Images

Write your answers.

1. You see an armadillo eating berries from a bush. What would you conclude?

_____

2. You are searching for armadillos in the wild. What kind of ground should you look for?

_____

Use It

Read about this toy. What can you conclude about it?

BUILDER BLOCKS

Builder Blocks are building toys that grow with a child. The first set, Red Builder, is a simple bag of building blocks. The blocks fit together in clever ways. Even small children can enjoy playing with these. Other sets become more complicated, until the child reaches Rainbow Builder. In this set, each block holds an electric device, so the child can build structures that move. Even so, the blocks still fit together with the ones from the child's first Red Builder set.

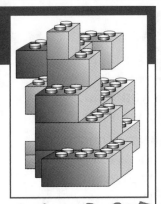

Write your answers.

1. Which set would be a good choice for a child of 3 or 4 who is just beginning to develop motor skills?

_____

2. Which set would be a good choice for a girl of 12 who is becoming interested in machines?

_____

Filling Gaps

♦ *Making Inferences*

Sometimes writers leave things out. They may leave out important points, even the main point. As you read, make good guesses about what's missing. In your mind, fill any gaps the writer may have left.

This Is the Idea

Read this part of a geography text and think about the writer's point.

Australia

Australia is one of the hottest, driest, flattest places on Earth. About a third of this country is desert, and some temperatures have reached almost 130 degrees. No wonder so few people live there. All of Australia has fewer than 20 million people. It has almost 120 million sheep.

The writer has told you about the climate in Australia and about people and animals that live there. Those details are in blue ink. From them, you can infer that this climate is not ideal for humans. You can also infer that sheep thrive in this climate.

As you read, ask yourself

- Can I connect ideas to come up with new ones?
- Do my new ideas make sense, based on what I read?

Take a Closer Look

Read this shopping tip and think about the writer's point.

Careful Shoppers Choose Chicken

A roasting chicken may seem to be expensive at first. Yet a five-pound bird can provide many meals for a family. The first night, roast the bird and serve it hot. The next day, slice the leftovers for hot or cold sandwiches. The third day, make creamed chicken or chicken salad from the bits and pieces. You can then use the skin, bones, and scraps to make soup.

Which of these is a good guess about the costs of chicken? **Hint:** Think about why the writer says "at first." Circle your answer.

a. Chickens are the best source of meat for sandwiches.

b. Chickens are a good value since they provide many meals.

Try It

Read this travel tip and think about the writer's point.

Enjoying Regional Foods

Travelers should make a point of trying the regional foods that are served in each state. Most of the time, those foods are made from local produce, and are very fresh and tasty. So the next time you are in Maine, eat blueberries. When you go to the Carolinas, try sweet potato rolls or sweet potato pie.

Write your answers.

1. From what you can infer, which state grows blueberries?

   _____

2. From what you can infer, where are sweet potatoes grown?

   _____

3. From what you know and can infer, name somewhere to find good fresh-squeezed orange juice.

   _____

Use It

As you read this science text, think about the writer's point.

Horned Toads

Texas horned toads do have horns, but otherwise their name is misleading. These small animals are about the same size as toads, and like toads, they have squat, bumpy bodies. However, Texas horned toads are really lizards, which are reptiles. Reptiles have dry, scaly skin and can survive in deserts. True toads are amphibians, which have moist skin and must live near water.

Write your answers.

1. From what you can infer, how did horned toads get their name?

   _____

2. From what you can infer, where should you look for a true toad?

   _____

3. From what you can infer, where should you look for a horned toad?

   _____

Using Good Guesses

◆ *Applying Inferences*

An inference is a good guess about something that the writer suggests but does not say. (See Lesson 26.) You can use inferences to learn more about a topic. You can also use them to learn about related topics.

This Is the Idea

Read this part of a text about pandas, and think about the main point.

How Many Giant Pandas Are Left?

There are few giant pandas left in the world, though no one knows exact numbers. Wild pandas now live in a few widely scattered areas in China. Most times, pandas within an area live completely alone. Scientists usually see only panda droppings and resting places. The animals are shy and good at staying out of sight.

The main point is that no one knows exactly how many giant pandas are left. The writer tells you some facts about pandas. From these, you can infer—make a good guess—that scientists probably have trouble counting wild pandas because they do not often see them.

Take a Closer Look

As you read, ask yourself

- Do some ideas suggest other ideas?
- Can I use those new ideas to extend what the writer says?

Read this health tip for parents, and think about the writer's point.

Save Those Baby Teeth

Your child needs baby teeth for years, so take care of them. Don't put a baby to bed with a bottle of juice or milk. During a nap, the sugar in these drinks stays on baby's teeth for hours. Sugar harms the teeth and can even cause tooth loss. Give cool water to babies who need naptime bottles.

1. Which of these is a good guess about naptime bottles? Circle it.
   a. Water will not harm a baby's teeth.
   b. Water will harm a baby's teeth just as juice or milk will.

2. Based on what you read, which is a good guess? Circle it.
   a. Do not give babies water more than once a day.
   b. Do not put sugar on a baby's pacifier.

Try It

Read this cooking tip and think about the writer's point.

Sift Before You Measure

Many baking recipes call for flour. To get good results, sift flour before measuring unless the recipe says not to. Then spoon the flour into a measuring cup, heaping it a bit. Use a knife edge to scrape off the flour above the rim. Sifted flour contains air, so one cup holds less than a cup of unsifted flour.

Circle your answers.

1. Which of these is a good guess about sifting flour?
   a. Recipes always tell you if you need to sift flour.
   b. A recipe may not succeed if you don't sift flour first.

2. Based on what you read, which of these is also a good guess?
   a. You may add too much flour if you do not sift it first.
   b. You may add too little flour if you do not sift it first.

Use It

Read this travel tip and think about the writer's point.

What to Do in Florida

Florida offers plenty of warmth and water, so take advantage of both. With an ocean on one side and a gulf on the other, this state is a boater's paradise. The state also has many lakes, rivers, and canals. Since boat rentals and boat ramps are common, you won't have any trouble sailing or canoeing.

Write your answers.

1. Would you guess that people in Florida are more likely to own boats than people in other states or less likely?

   _____

2. Would Florida be a good vacation spot if you like water skiing?

   _____

3. Would Florida be a good place to open a shop to sell mittens?

   _____

Getting the Big Picture

◆ *Making Generalizations*

As you read, pause now and then to step back from the details. Think about the general meaning of the text. If you can, write a general statement about the details.

This Is the Idea

Look at this graph. What can you say in general about it?

What can you say about the details in the graph? You can say that traffic is heavier in the fall and winter than it is in the spring and summer. You can say that at least 20,000 cars come to the city daily.

Take a Closer Look

Ask yourself
- What is the general idea?
- If the writer doesn't state one, can I make a good guess at one?

Read this article. What can you say in general about it?

Television and Schoolwork

A recent survey studied TV and schoolwork. Children who watch TV during dinner do not do as well in school as those who don't watch. Children who watch TV before bed do not do as well in school as those who don't watch. On the other hand, children who play games and read tend to do better in school.

Which is the best general statement about the details? Circle your answer. **Hint:** Your statement has to be true about all the survey results stated.

a. For children, watching TV during dinner is linked to poorer school work, and so is watching TV before bed.

b. For children, watching TV is linked to poorer schoolwork, but playing games and reading are linked to better schoolwork.

Try It

What can you say in general about the month's weather?

Last Month's Weather Summary	Days with high temperatures above average 21
	Days with high temperatures below average 9
	Days with rainfall above average...6
	Days with rainfall below average.....................................24
	Sunny days...25
	Cloudy days..5

Circle your answers.

1. In general, how would you describe last month's rainfall?
   a. drier than average
   b. wetter than average

2. In general, how would you describe last month's temperature?
   a. cooler than average
   b. warmer than average

Write your answer.

3. In general, how would you describe the month's weather?

   _____

Use It

Read this cookbook and decide what to say in general about pans.

Choosing Pans

You can get pans made of stainless steel, aluminum, copper, or cast iron. My personal choice is stainless steel. It's the easiest to clean and lasts forever. When you're trying to choose between two pans, knock on the bottom of each. The thicker, sturdier one will make a solid sound, not a tinny sound. Choose that one for longest life and best quality.

Write your answers.

1. What does the writer say in general about stainless steel?

   _____

2. What can you say in general about choosing between two pans?

   _____

Checking the Big Picture

◆ *Testing Generalizations*

This Is the Idea

Read this part of a letter. What can you say in general about it?

> Dear Alisha,
>
> We've been camping in the desert south of Tucson. The days have been warm, but at night the temperature falls quickly. As the sun sets, the night sky fills with stars, more than I've ever seen before. You have the feeling that you could touch the moon, and its light is very bright.

You could say, in general, that nights in the desert south of Tucson are much cooler than days. **You could also say that** the night air is very clear and there aren't a lot of electric lights.

Take a Closer Look

Ask yourself

- Does the general statement fit the facts?
- Does it cover all the facts?
- Does it make sense or does it go too far?
- Is it fair?

Read this part of a sports report. What can you say in general about it?

> Ned Michaels took a huge risk when he decided to come out of retirement and join the Reston Ramblers. The young team had a dismal record, and Michaels had every chance of looking like an old man long past his prime. Instead, he has brought leadership to the youngsters, and they seem to have given him a second wind. Together, they're winning.

Which general statement fits the facts but doesn't go too far? Circle your answer. *Hint:* One statement fits the old and young players in general.

a. Ned Michaels is the only reason the Reston Ramblers are winning.

b. The young players help Michaels out when he's in a tight spot.

c. Michaels's experience and the other players' youth have made a team that's hard to beat.

d. Older players are the key to more exciting basketball games.

Try It

Think about the writer's general statement in this review.

Annual Fair Flops

This year's River City Fair has ended, and it was not as successful as past fairs. There were no new rides this year and no new games or acts. There weren't even any new food stalls. More people attended than ever before.

Write your answers.

1. How many people attended the fair?

   _____

2. What general statement does the writer make?

   _____

3. What statement suggests that the general statement is wrong?

   _____

Use It

Think about the writer's general statements in this health article.

Herb Tea and Health

The studies show that herb tea is good for your health. In one study, people who drank herb tea got fewer colds than people who did not drink herb tea. Another study found that people who drank herb tea had fewer colds than people who drank coffee. Other studies have not shown clear results. In one, people who drank water had fewer colds than those who drank herb tea.

Write your answers.

1. The writer says, "The studies show that herb tea is good for your health." What is wrong with that general statement?

   _____

2. What would be a better general statement?

   _____

   _____

Finding the Facts

◆ *Separating Fact from Opinion*

A fact is true and can be proved in some way. An opinion cannot be proved, since it is what someone feels or believes. Different people have different feelings and beliefs, but facts are true for everyone.

This Is the Idea

Which parts of this club newsletter are statements of fact?

> # Garden Club Plant Sale
>
> Last month, our Garden Club held its plant sale at Yarrow Hall. This sale was more fun than ever! Two thousand visitors enjoyed our beautiful displays. They bought plants from 24 vendors and attended nine workshops. Proceeds from this sale were used to buy flowering bulbs for City Hall.

You could prove the statements in black ink. You could check the time and place in a local paper, ticket stubs would show how many people attended, and the club's records would show where the money was spent.

You can't prove that this sale was more fun than ever or that the displays were beautiful. Those are the writer's opinions. Others might not agree.

Take a Closer Look

Here are ways that you can check statements of fact:

- You can observe— see with your own eyes—that it is true.
- You can check it in a reliable source.

Which parts of this travel piece are statements of fact?

> # Wacky Festivals
>
> The United States has a great number of wacky festivals. At least once a month, one state will have one. May brings a Bed Race and a Barbed Wire Swap, June has a Chicken Clucking Contest, July has a Lawnmower Riding Race, and a Bathtub Race is in the fall. Any of these would be fun to see.

Circle your answers. Remember that you can prove a fact by checking a good source. An opinion tells what someone believes.

1. What kind of statement is the second sentence?
   a. fact   b. opinion

2. What kind of statement is the last sentence?
   a. fact   b. opinion

Try It

Which parts of this profile are opinions?

The Four Freedoms

In 1943, painter Norman Rockwell showed four pictures. They are called *Freedom of Speech, Freedom of Worship, Freedom from Want,* and *Freedom from Fear.* These are some of the most moving of his works. They show scenes that every person has experienced. Rockwell said he liked the first two best.

Put a check mark in front of each opinion. Remember, an opinion tells what someone feels or believes.

_____ a. In 1943, Norman Rockwell published four pictures.

_____ b. These are some of the most moving of his works.

_____ c. They show scenes that every person has experienced.

_____ d. Rockwell said he liked the first two best.

Use It

Which parts of this article are facts? Which part is opinion?

The First Woman Voter

In 1868, a woman voted for a U.S. president for the first time. Charlotte Parkhurst cast that vote. This was illegal at the time. Women did not have the right to vote then. She was disguised as a man and used the name Charlie. What an exciting life she lived! She drove a stagecoach and fought off outlaws, and no one knew she was a woman until she died.

Write one fact and one opinion from this article.

1. Fact: _____

_____

2. Opinion: _____

_____

Thinking about Opinions

◆ *Evaluating Opinions*

An opinion is what someone feels or believes. Reasonable opinions are backed up by facts and research. They are backed up by good reasons. Look for reasons and facts when you judge an opinion.

This Is the Idea

Look for facts and opinions in this editorial from a neighborhood paper.

> ### Helmet Rule a Mistake
>
> Local students who ride bikes to school must now wear helmets. Students without them will not be allowed to ride their bikes home. Bike helmets are a good idea, but they should not be required. **Many students have no helmets or don't like wearing them.** They shouldn't be penalized.

The writer uses facts in the first two sentences. The sentences in blue ink state opinions. The sentence in bold type states reasons for the writer's opinions. You do not learn any reasons for the school's new rule, though. Do you have enough facts to judge the writer's opinion?

Take a Closer Look

When you read an opinion, ask

- Does the writer support opinions with facts and reasons?
- Does the writer give all the important facts?

Read this part of a letter to the editor. Think about the writer's opinion.

> New Rule Is Good
>
> I think that your editorial is just plain wrong. For one thing, you're not giving students credit for good sense. Students are smart enough to know the value of bike helmets. Last year, 97 percent of bike riders killed in accidents were not wearing helmets. No one should ride without a helmet.

Write your answers.

1. What does the writer think about riders and helmets?

_____

2. What is one reason or fact that the writer gives?

_____

Try It

Read this part of a letter to the editor. Think about the writer's opinion.

Helmet Laws Work

Figures show that helmet laws reduce injuries and deaths. Today, 20 states have helmet laws. New Jersey passed a law 10 years ago. Later, deaths for one age group dropped by 60 percent. Other state laws produced similar effects. These results should convince you that our helmet rule should stay.

Write your answers.

1. What is the writer's opinion of the helmet rule?

   _____

2. What facts does the writer give to support this opinion?

   _____

   _____

   _____

Use It

Read this editorial and think about the writer's opinion.

The Last Word on Helmet Rule

Readers have sent a dozen letters about the helmet law. This rule does deprive riders of some freedom. But students must follow many rules that adults don't. Currently, just a few student riders wear helmets. This rule will increase that number. Therefore, the new rule should stand.

Write your answers.

1. What is the writer's opinion?

   _____

2. Do the writer's reasons make this opinion seem reasonable?

   _____

3. Why do you think as you do?

   _____

Answer Key

Lesson 1

Take a Closer Look
1. b   2. b

Try It
1. a   2. b

Use It
1. a   2. b   3. b   4. a

Lesson 2

Take a Closer Look
1. a   2. b

Try It
1. tense
2. pleased

Use It
1. stuffed full
2. discouraged
3. weed out

Lesson 3

Take a Closer Look
a, c

Try It
1. b   2. b

Use It
1. quickly
2. slowly

Lesson 4

Take a Closer Look
1. chemists
2. They combined some of the best qualities of oils and watercolors.

Try It
1. on the side of your neck, just below the jawbone
2. after you've been working out for a few weeks (if you're young and healthy)

Use It
1. a network of computer networks
2. often by cables or phone wires
3. communicate with one another
4. anyone who is linked

Lesson 5

Take a Closer Look
1. Answers will vary but should come from column 1.
2. Answers will vary but should come from column 2.

Try It
1. should be added under What I Already Know
2. should be added under What I Want to Know
3. Answers will vary but should be listed under What I Already Know.
4. Answers will vary but should be listed under What I Want to Know.

Use It
Answers will vary but should be listed under What I Learned.

Lesson 6

Take a Closer Look
a, c

Try It
b

Use It
c

Lesson 7

Take a Closer Look

a

Try It

a

Use It

Answers may vary.

1. find a barber who needed a checkup
2. trading for goods and services

Lesson 8

Take a Closer Look

1. before ordering shades
2. measuring for shades

Try It

1. yes
2. no
3. buying a chicken to cook

Use It

1. yes
2. pictures or paintings
3. the National Portrait Gallery

Lesson 9

Take a Closer Look

The trick to getting pets to stay still is feeding them.
or
Others are calmer with the owners away.

Try It

2. Don't look only at the package price.
   Compare the cost per ounce and the cost per portion.
   The unit-pricing label will help.

Use It

1. the United States Supreme Court
2. The United States Supreme Court is the highest court in the country.
   It is made up of one Chief Justice and eight associate justices.
   The Supreme Court tries only cases that affect the laws of the nation.

Lesson 10

Take a Closer Look

1. b
2. The inclined plane is a simple machine that makes work easier.

Try It

1. b
2. Pollen makes many people sneeze.

Use It

In the end, Anthony won her struggle for women's rights, though she wasn't alive to see it.

Lesson 11

Take a Closer Look

b

Try It

1. a   2. b

Use It

1. b
2. Answers will vary.

Lesson 12

Take a Closer Look

b, d

Try It

1. Be sure the whites contain no yolk.
2. Eggs at room temperature work better than icy ones.
3. Beat egg whites in a clean, deep bowl, and use them at once.

Use It

Answers will vary.

Lesson 13

Take a Closer Look

c, d

Try It

1. Don't use your real name on the Internet.
2. Don't tell anyone online where you live or go to school.
3. Don't meet an online friend without permission.

Use It

1. Cameras were large and hard to use.
2. It let people take pictures by just pressing a button.
3. Cameras were selling by the thousands.

Lesson 14

Take a Closer Look

a

Try It

1, 3, 4, 2

Use It

1. a
2. a
3. Press the cover until it snaps into place.

Lesson 15

Take a Closer Look

1. the onions
2. crunchy

Try It

You might buy too much wire or not enough.

Use It

1. The water in the lock might not match the level outside the gate.
2. The water would pour through the lock from the high-water side to the low-water side.

Lesson 16

Take a Closer Look

2. because glass doesn't let radiant heat through it

Try It

1. A light bulb burned out.
2. A fuse burned out or a circuit breaker was tripped.

Use It

1. They can't see that it will do them any good in the real world.
2. Invite your child to help when you have practical math work to do.

Lesson 17

Take a Closer Look

1. to kill bacteria
2. Bacteria from the chicken might get on the roll.

Try It

1. It makes a chirp.
2. mainly to attract female crickets

Use It

1. Eat less and be more active.
2. about 2 pounds
   (1,000 calories a day adds up to 7,000 calories a week. 3,500 calories equals about a pound, so 7,000 calories equals about 2 pounds.)

Lesson 18

Take a Closer Look

because they will stain

Try It

Business Math

Use It

1. $600.00   2. $0.00   3. 27%

Lesson 19

Take a Closer Look

hotel and restaurant

Try It

pug dogs

Use It

1. Chapter 1
2. Chapter 3

Lesson 20

Take a Closer Look

1. It is larger and brighter.
2. It is easier to get to.
3. It doesn't have the charm that the old building had.

Try It

1. a   2. b

Use It

1. Poppers
2. Poppers
3. Poppers

Lesson 21

Take a Closer Look

1. Plan 1
2. Plan 2

Try It

1. Bob Counts
2. Bob Saves the Day

Use It

1. because it looks better and doesn't cost much
2. chain-link

Lesson 22

Take a Closer Look

The report will be done on time.

Try It

1. People will go to the other shops.
2. People will come to your shop.

Use It

1. The honey bee will die.
2. The colony will fail.

Lesson 23

Take a Closer Look

a

Try It

1. They will refuse to do it.
2. You will get only one.

Use It

1. lower
2. yours

Lesson 24

Take a Closer Look

c

Try It

1. animal power
2. in the Middle East

Use It

1. They don't always agree.
2. It depends on your body's needs.

Lesson 25

Take a Closer Look

1. *Computer Monthly*
2. Answers will vary.

Try It

1. The armadillo couldn't find any insects to eat.
2. ground that is loose enough for the armadillo to dig a burrow in

Use It

1. Red Builder
2. Rainbow Builder

Lesson 26

Take a Closer Look

b

Try It

1. Maine
2. in North and South Carolina
3. Answers will vary.

Use It

1. from their appearance, because they look like toads and have horns
2. near a stream or pond
3. in a desert

Lesson 27

Take a Closer Look

1. a   2. b

Try It

1. b   2. a

Use It

1. more likely
2. yes
3. no

Lesson 28

Take a Closer Look

b

Try It

1. a
2. b
3. It was sunny and was warmer and drier than normal.

Use It

1. It's easy to clean and lasts forever.
2. The thicker, sturdier one is better quality and will last longer.

Lesson 29

Take a Closer Look

c

Try It

1. more than ever before
2. It was not as successful as past fairs.
3. More people attended than ever before.

Use It

1. It goes too far.
2. Two studies suggest that herb tea may help prevent colds.

Lesson 30

Take a Closer Look

1. a   2. b

Try It

b, c

Use It

1. Answers will vary.
2. What an exciting life she lived!

Lesson 31

Take a Closer Look

1. No one should ride without a helmet.
2. Last year, 97 percent of bike riders killed in accidents were not wearing helmets.

Try It

1. The helmet rule should stay.
2. Today, 20 states have helmet laws. New Jersey passed a law 10 years ago. Later, deaths for one age group dropped by 60 percent. Other state laws produced similar results.

Use It

1. The new rule should stand.
2. Answers will vary.
3. Answers will vary.